Junior Great Books®

Reader's Journal

Series 5   Book One

This book belongs to:

_____

The Great Books Foundation
A nonprofit educational organization

The interpretive discussion program that moves
students toward excellence in reading comprehension,
critical thinking, and writing

9 8 7 6
Printed in the United States of America

Cover art by Terea Shaffer. Copyright 2006 by Terea Shaffer.
Text and cover design by William Seabright, William Seabright & Associates.
Interior design by Think Design Group.

Published and distributed by

The Great Books Foundation
A nonprofit educational organization
35 East Wacker Drive, Suite 400
Chicago, IL 60601

SUSTAINABLE FORESTRY INITIATIVE   Certified Fiber Sourcing
Label applies to the text stock   www.sfiprogram.org

Welcome to Your Reader's Journal

This Reader's Journal is a place for you to collect your thoughts about the Junior Great Books stories you read and discuss in class. Here, you can be an artist and a poet, while discovering some secrets to becoming a strong reader and writer.

There are many parts of the Reader's Journal to explore:

Writing Notebook allows you to gather some of your favorite pieces of writing in one place to revise and polish them.

Curious Words is where you can record the strange or interesting words you come across while reading. You don't have to memorize these words—you get to play with them, sounding them out in your head or out loud or using them to make up messages and rhymes.

The **glossary** contains unusual or difficult words from the stories you've read. Look here for definitions that will help you better understand what you are reading.

Are you hunting for a **keeper question**, or do you have your **Head in the Clouds**? Maybe you're **Building Your Answer**, **Writing to Explain** or **Explore**, or getting **Into Reading**. Whatever you're working on, this Reader's Journal belongs to you. It's the place for your great ideas.

Contents

The No-Guitar Blues   **1**
Gary Soto

Kaddo's Wall   **11**
West African folktale as told by
Harold Courlander and George Herzog

Turquoise Horse   **21**
Gerald Hausman

A Game of Catch   **31**
Richard Wilbur

Oliver Hyde's Dishcloth Concert   **43**
Richard Kennedy

The Hundred-Dollar Bill   **53**
from On the Way Home, Rose Wilder Lane

The Invisible Child   **65**
Tove Jansson

In the Time of the Drums   **77**
Gullah folktale as told by Kim L. Siegelson

Learning the Game   **87**
from The Circuit, Francisco Jiménez

The Bat-Poet   **99**
Randall Jarrell

Writing Notebook   **111**

Curious Words   **125**

Glossary   **137**

The No-Guitar Blues

Gary Soto

Asking questions is an important part of understanding what you're reading. Read the following two passages from the story and write a question that you have about each one. Remember your questions as you read the story a second time to help you understand the story better.

Your questions might be about:

- Why a character does or says something
- Why something happens the way it does
- What a word, phrase, or sentence means
- A place where you feel confused about what is happening

PASSAGE 1 (page 12)

Fausto looked at the bill and knew he was in trouble. Not with these nice folks or with his parents but with himself. How could he be so deceitful? The dog wasn't lost. It was just having a fun Saturday walking around.

Your question about this passage:

_____

_____

_____

_____

PASSAGE 2 (page 14)

Fausto knelt, prayed, and sang. But he couldn't forget the man and the lady, whose names he didn't even know, and the *empanada* they had given him.

Your question about this passage:

_____

_____

_____

_____

PASSAGE 3 (page _____)

Copy a passage from the story that you marked with a **?** below.

_____

_____

_____

_____

_____

Your question about this passage:

_____

_____

_____

_____

_____

Head in the Clouds

Use your imagination! Choose one of the topics in the clouds and draw a picture or write a little bit more about the story.

My favorite part of the story

Something that the story reminds me of

An advertisement Fausto could put up in his neighborhood to earn money

What I would do if I found a lost pet

Building Your Answer

The focus question:

_____

_____

_____

_____

Your answer before the discussion:

_____

_____

_____

_____

Your answer after the discussion _(you may change or add to your first answer)_**:**

_____

_____

_____

_____

_____

Writing to Explain

Look at your answer after the discussion on page 5. Now underline a part of your answer that you can say more about. After you think about how to make your answer more detailed, write the new one below.

Your new answer:

_____

_____

_____

_____

_____

_____

Writing to Explore

Prewriting Notes

Below, write down some things that Fausto could do to earn money
during each season of the year.

Spring

Summer

Fall

Winter

Writing to Explore

Now select one idea from each box on page 7 and explain, in more detail, how Fausto could put each idea into action.

An Idea For . . .	How to Do It
Spring	
Summer	
Fall	
Winter	

Writing to Explore A Plan for Fausto

Writing a Draft

Now write your one-year plan for Fausto to earn money, using complete, detailed sentences.

A Plan for Fausto

_____

_____

_____

_____

_____

_____

_____

_____

_____

_____

_____

_____

_____

_____

_____

_____

_____

_____

_____

Writing to Explore

A Plan for Fausto

Use this page if you need more room.

Kaddo's Wall

West African folktale
as told by Harold Courlander
and George Herzog

In the space below, write a **keeper question** about the story that came into your mind during the first reading, while sharing questions, or even right now. Choose one that no one has completely answered yet, and keep it in your mind during the second reading. If you still have the question after reading, continue to think about it—you picked a real keeper!

Your keeper question:

_____

_____

_____

_____

Asking questions is an important part of understanding what you're reading. Read the following passages from the story and write a question that you have about each one. Remember your questions when you read the story a second time to help you understand the story better.

Your questions might be about:

- Why a character does or says something

- Why something happens the way it does

- What a word, phrase, or sentence means

- A place where you feel confused about what is happening

PASSAGE 1 (page 20)

And now when people came to see him they had to stand by the gate until he asked them to enter. When the workers who plowed and planted for Kaddo wanted to talk to him, Kaddo sat on the wall by the gate and listened to them and gave them orders.

Your question about this passage:

_____

_____

_____

_____

Into Reading

Asking Questions

PASSAGE 2 (page 23)

"But tell me, there was a rich and powerful man in Tendella named Kaddo, wasn't there? What ever happened to him? Is he still alive?" [Sogole asked.]

"Yes, he is still alive," Kaddo said.

Your question about this passage:

_____

_____

_____

_____

PASSAGE 3 (page _____)

Copy a passage from the story that you marked with a **?** below.

_____

_____

_____

_____

_____

Your question about this passage:

_____

_____

_____

_____

Head in the Clouds

Use your imagination! Choose one of the topics in the clouds and draw a picture or write a little bit more about the story.

My favorite
part of
the story

A picture of
Kaddo sitting
on his wall

A letter to the
people of Seno

A sentence from
the story that I liked,
and why

Building Your Answer

The focus question:

_____

_____

_____

_____

Your answer before the discussion:

_____

_____

_____

_____

Your answer after the discussion _(you may change or add to your first answer)_:

_____

_____

_____

_____

_____

Writing to Explain   Introducing Your Evidence

Prewriting Notes

Write your answer after the discussion from the Building Your Answer page (page 15) in the top box. Then complete the web by selecting pieces of evidence that support your main idea and writing them in the other boxes.

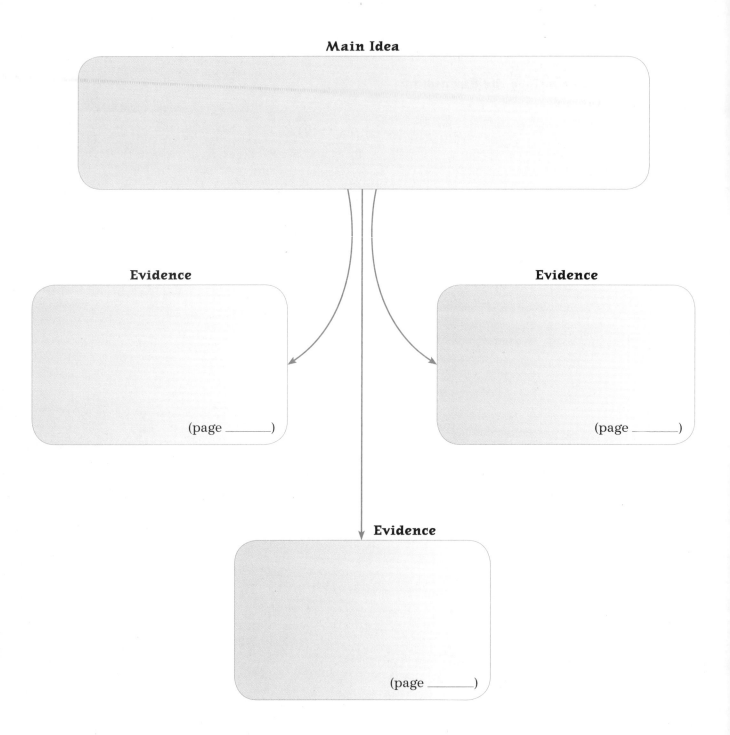

Main Idea

Evidence

(page _____)

Evidence

(page _____)

Evidence

(page _____)

Writing to Explain Introducing Your Evidence

Writing a Draft

Now turn your web into a paragraph, using complete, detailed sentences.

Writing to Explore   A Letter of Advice

Prewriting Notes

If you were one of the common people who lived in Seno, how would you explain the phrase "Don't build a wall of flour around your house" to a rich person? Below, list some ideas for your letter.

To me, the phrase "Don't build a wall of flour around your house" means

_____

_____

_____

_____

I think it means this because

_____

_____

_____

_____

This advice is important to follow because

_____

_____

_____

_____

Writing to Explore

Writing a Draft

Write your letter in the space below. Remember to include a salutation and a closing.

Turquoise Horse

by Gerald Hausman

In the space below, write a keeper question about the story that came into your mind during the first reading, while sharing questions, or even right now. Choose one that no one has completely answered yet, and keep it in your mind during the second reading. If you still have the question after reading, continue to think about it—you picked a real keeper!

Your keeper question:

_____

_____

_____

_____

Asking questions is an important part of understanding what you're reading. Read the following two passages from the story and write a question that you have about each one. Remember your questions as you read the story a second time to help you understand the story better.

Your questions might be about:

- Why a character does or says something

- Why something happens the way it does

- What a word, phrase, or sentence means

- A place where you feel confused about what is happening

PASSAGE 1 (page 30)

"You know it is a bad thing to disturb the sacred places of burial. I did nothing with the bracelet. I merely looked at it. I took it with my eyes, for a moment, and held it there."

Your question about this passage:

_____

_____

_____

PASSAGE 2 (page 31)

"The thing that made the bracelet so beautiful was the turquoise horse that decorated it. I've never forgotten that horse that seemed to be dancing on a cloud."

Your question about this passage:

_____

_____

_____

PASSAGE 3 (page _____)

Copy a passage from the story that you marked with a **?** below.

_____

_____

_____

_____

Your question about this passage:

_____

_____

_____

Head in the Clouds

Use your imagination! Choose one of the topics in the clouds and draw a picture or write a little bit more about the story.

A pictur
of Lisa riding
the turquois
horse

A dream tha
I remembe
very well

Something that
my keeper
question makes
me think about

Words to a song
that I'd give
John Arrowsmith
to sing

Building Your Answer

The focus question:

_____

_____

_____

_____

Your answer before the discussion:

_____

_____

_____

_____

Your answer after the discussion _(you may change or add to your first answer)_:

_____

_____

_____

_____

_____

Include one piece of evidence from the story that supports your answer, using your own words.

_____

_____

_____

_____

_____

Writing to Explain Explaining Your Evidence

Prewriting Notes

Write your answer after the discussion from your Building Your Answer page
(page 25) in the top box. Then write supporting evidence in the other boxes.
Think about how your evidence supports the main idea, and then write those
explanations in the space provided.

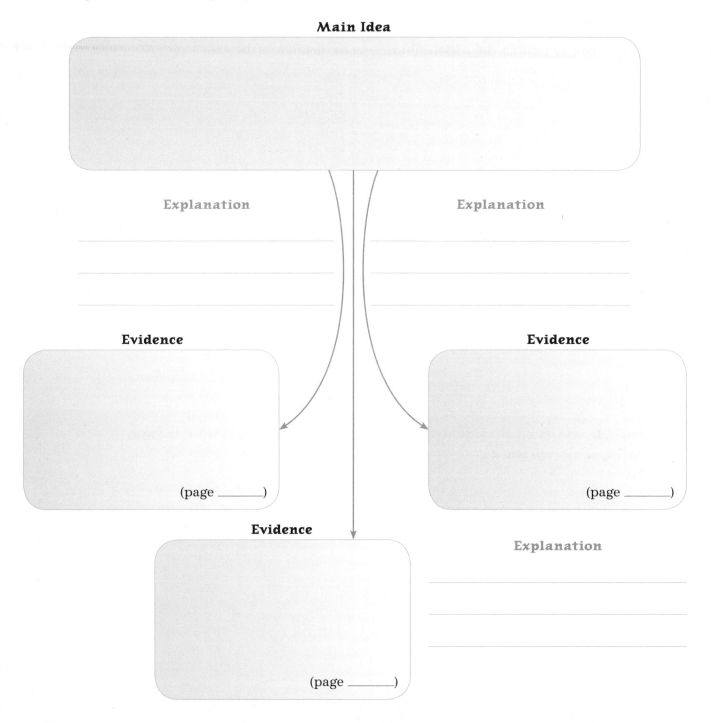

Main Idea

Explanation

Explanation

Evidence

(page _____)

Evidence

(page _____)

Evidence

(page _____)

Explanation

Writing to Explain

Writing a Draft

Now write your essay using your prewriting notes, explaining how your evidence supports your main idea. Give your essay an interesting title.

_____

_____

_____

_____

_____

_____

_____

_____

_____

_____

_____

_____

_____

_____

_____

_____

_____

_____

Writing to Explain   Explaining Your Evidence

Use this page if you need more room.

_____

_____

_____

_____

_____

_____

_____

_____

_____

_____

_____

_____

_____

_____

_____

_____

_____

_____

_____

_____

_____

_____

Writing to Explore   Your Symbolic Object

Prewriting Notes

Think about an object that is a *symbol* to you. It may be something you own, or it may belong to someone else. It may be found in nature or in your house, or it may be a public object, such as a building, a statue, or a painting.

A **symbol** is a thing used to represent something else—often something invisible or untouchable, such as an emotion or an idea.

Your symbol:

_____

What this object symbolizes to you:

_____

_____

_____

_____

_____

Why this object is symbolic:

_____

_____

_____

_____

_____

Writing to Explore

Writing Your Draft

Below, using your prewriting notes, write a paragraph or a poem about your symbol, explaining what it symbolizes to you, and why.

_____

_____

_____

_____

_____

_____

_____

_____

_____

_____

_____

_____

_____

_____

_____

_____

_____

_____

_____

A Game of Catch

Richard Wilbur

In the space below, write a keeper question about the story that came into your mind during the first reading, while sharing questions, or even right now. Choose one that no one has completely answered yet, and keep it in your mind during the second reading. If you still have the question after reading, continue to think about it—you picked a real keeper!

Your keeper question:

_____

_____

_____

_____

Connecting your knowledge and personal experience to a story can help you make better sense of it.

Look in the story for places where you marked a **C**. Below, use your own words to describe what happened in the story. Then explain how that part of the story **connects** to something you know about or experienced in your own life, and how your connection helps you understand something in the story or about life.

Something that happens in the story:

_____

_____

_____

_____

Your connection:

_____

_____

_____

_____

How your connection helps you better understand something in the story or about life (circle one):

_____

_____

_____

_____

Something that happens in the story:

_____

_____

_____

_____

Your connection:

_____

_____

_____

_____

**How your connection helps you better understand something
in the story or something about life** (circle one):

_____

_____

_____

_____

Head in the Clouds

Use your imagination! Choose one of the topics in the clouds and draw a picture or write a little bit more about the story.

A picture or description of Scho in the tree

A picture or description of the most interesting scene

Why I liked / did not like this story

A time that I felt left out or teased, and what I did about it

Building Your Answer

The focus question:

_____

_____

_____

_____

Your answer before the discussion:

_____

_____

_____

_____

Your answer after the discussion (you may change or add to your first answer):

_____

_____

_____

_____

An idea you heard in the discussion that helped you:

_____

_____

_____

_____

Writing to Explain   Two Sides of the Story

Prewriting Notes

Does Scho fall from the tree on purpose? Find some evidence from the story to support each answer to the question.

Scho falls from the tree *on purpose.*

Evidence:

_____

_____

_____

_____

_____

_____

_____

Scho falls from the tree *by accident.*

Evidence:

_____

_____

_____

_____

_____

_____

_____

Writing to Explain

Writing a Draft

Below, write your essay, giving evidence for both answers to the question.
End the essay by explaining which answer you agree with and why.

Introduction
(your main idea)

_____

_____

_____

_____

_____

_____

_____

_____

_____

**Why it seems
that Scho falls
on purpose**

_____

_____

_____

_____

_____

_____

_____

continue ⟶

Writing to Explain

Why it seems that Scho falls by accident

_____

_____

_____

_____

_____

_____

_____

_____

My own answer to the question, and why I chose that answer

_____

_____

_____

_____

_____

_____

_____

Conclusion (why your main idea is important to understand the story)

_____

_____

_____

_____

_____

_____

_____

Writing to Explore

Prewriting Notes

Imagine you are Scho, Glennie, or Monk. After the end of the story, where would you go? What would you say, and to whom? Below, write what you would do and how you would feel about each thing you do.

What I Would Do	How I Would Feel When I Do This
First:	
Then:	
Then:	

Writing to Explore

Writing a Draft

Using your prewriting notes, write three different paragraphs as if you are the character writing entries in his journal. Remember to include as much detail as you can about what you do and how you feel.

Oliver Hyde's Dishcloth Concert

by Richard Kennedy

In the space below, write a keeper question about the story that came into your mind during the first reading, while sharing questions, or even right now. Choose one that no one has completely answered yet, and keep it in your mind during the second reading. If you still have the question after reading, continue to think about it—you picked a real keeper!

Your keeper question:

_____

_____

_____

_____

Connecting your knowledge and personal experience to a story can help you make better sense of it.

Look in the story for places where you marked a **C**. Below, use your own words to describe what happened in the story. Then explain how that part of the story **connects** to something you know about or experienced in your own life, and how your connection helps you understand something in the story or about life.

Something that happens in the story:

_____

_____

_____

_____

Your connection:

_____

_____

_____

_____

**How your connection helps you better understand something
in the story or about life** (circle one):

_____

_____

_____

_____

Something that happens in the story:

_____

_____

_____

_____

Your connection:

_____

_____

_____

_____

How your connection helps you better understand something
in the story **or** about life (circle one):

_____

_____

_____

_____

Head in the Clouds

Use your imagination! Choose one of the topics in the clouds and draw a picture or write a little bit more about the story.

A picture of Oliver Hyde in my favorite scene

A letter to Oliver Hyde

A sentence from the story that I liked, and why

What I do when I'm sad about something

Building Your Answer

The focus question:

_____

_____

_____

_____

Your answer before the discussion:

_____

_____

_____

_____

Your answer after the discussion *(you may change or add to your first answer)*:

_____

_____

_____

_____

To support your answer, write down two quotes or brief passages from the story.

1. _____

_____

_____

2. _____

_____

_____

Writing to Explain   Concessions and Consequences

Prewriting Notes

In the boxes that follow, write Oliver Hyde's *concessions* and *consequences* in the order that they happen in the story.

A **concession** is made when someone allows something he or she normally wouldn't allow in order to reach an agreement or understanding with someone else. For example, Oliver makes a concession to play fiddle at the wedding if everyone wears a dishcloth on their heads.

A **consequence** is the result or effect of an action. For example, when everyone accepts Oliver's condition to wear a dishcloth, Oliver feels he is being tricked into playing. This is a consequence of his concession to play. He must keep his promise.

concession

consequence

concession

consequence

concession

consequence

Writing to Explain   Concessions and Consequences

Writing a Draft

Using your prewriting notes, draft a short essay answering this question:

> **Which of Oliver Hyde's concessions is the most important to how he changes in the story?**

Be sure to clearly explain Oliver's concession, how it changes Oliver, and why this is important to the story.

_____

_____

_____

_____

_____

_____

_____

_____

_____

_____

_____

_____

_____

_____

_____

_____

Writing to Explore

Prewriting Notes

Imagine what might have happened if Oliver were to first enter the barn where the wedding is being held instead of the empty one. Write these events and how you think Oliver might feel about each in the order you think they would happen.

Oliver enters the barn where the wedding is being held . . .

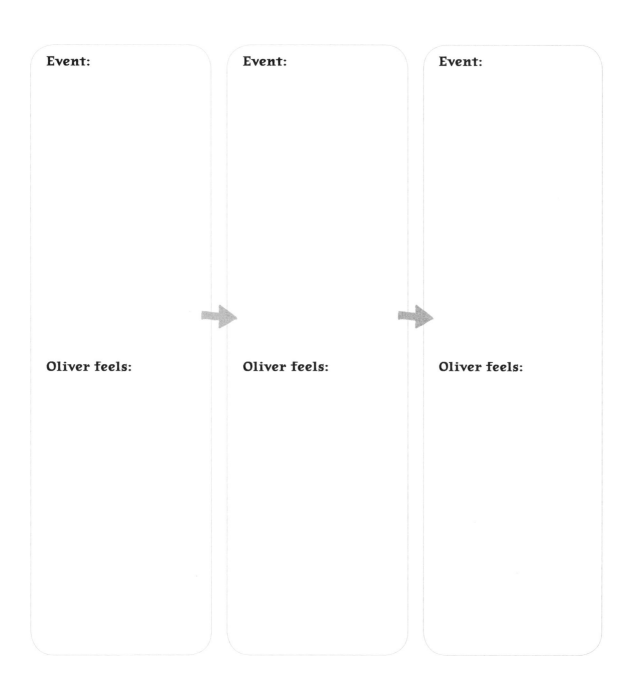

Event:

Event:

Event:

Oliver feels:

Oliver feels:

Oliver feels:

Writing to Explore

A New Ending

Writing a Draft

Now write your new ending to "Oliver Hyde's Dishcloth Concert," imagining what might have happened if Oliver had gone first to the barn where the wedding is being held. Use your prewriting notes to help you put the events in order and to provide details about how you think Oliver might feel about each event that happens. You may use the story as a model to help you write.

He entered Edward's barn with his hat pulled down and his collar turned up (page 143).

_____

_____

_____

_____

_____

_____

_____

_____

_____

_____

_____

_____

_____

_____

_____

_____

_____

_____

The Hundred-Dollar Bill

Rose Wilder Lane

In the space below, write a keeper question about the story that came into your mind during the first reading, while sharing questions, or even right now. Choose one that no one has completely answered yet, and keep it in your mind during the second reading. If you still have the question after reading, continue to think about it—you picked a real keeper!

Your keeper question:

_____

_____

_____

_____

Connecting your knowledge and personal experience to a story can help you make better sense of it.

Look in the story for places where you marked a **C**. Below, use your own words to describe what happened in the story. Then explain how that part of the story **connects** to something you know about or experienced in your own life, and how your connection helps you understand something in the story or about life.

Something that happens in the story:

_____

_____

_____

_____

Your connection:

_____

_____

_____

_____

How your connection helps you better understand something
in the story **or** about life (circle one):

_____

_____

_____

_____

Something that happens in the story:

_____

_____

_____

_____

Your connection:

_____

_____

_____

_____

How your connection helps you better understand something

in the story **or** about life (circle one):

_____

_____

_____

_____

Head in the Clouds

Use your imagination! Choose one of the topics in the clouds and draw a picture or write a little bit more about the story.

A map or drawing of the Sunday cam

Something from the story that makes me curious

A picture of Rose's mother

A letter to Rose

Building Your Answer

The focus question:

_____

_____

_____

_____

Your answer before the discussion:

_____

_____

_____

_____

Your answer after the discussion (you may change or add to your first answer):

_____

_____

_____

_____

_____

Writing to Explain   A Strong Introduction

Prewriting Notes

Use the web to map out your main idea and supporting evidence (the *body* of your essay). Explain your evidence in the space provided.

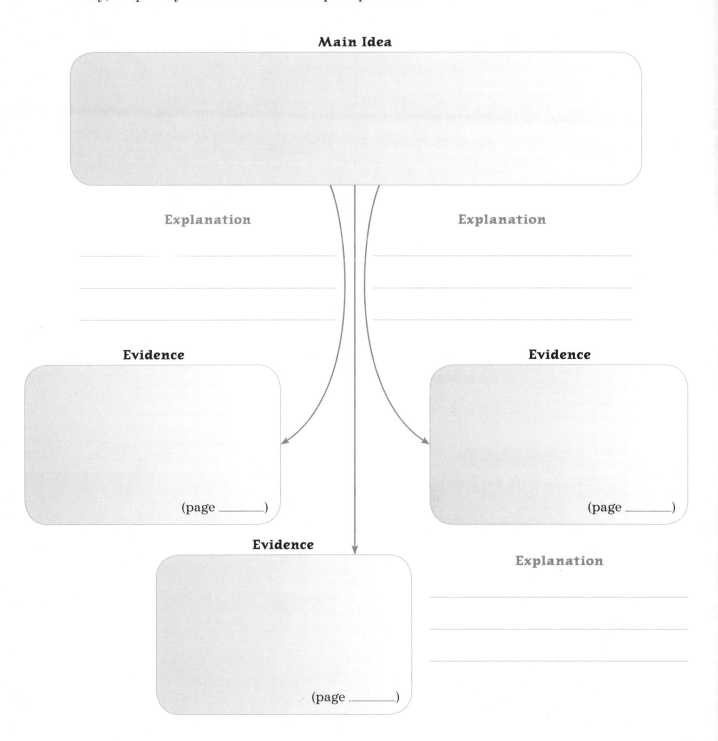

Main Idea

Explanation

Explanation

Evidence

Evidence

(page _____)

(page _____)

Evidence

Explanation

(page _____)

Writing to Explain   A Strong Introduction

Writing a Draft

Before drafting the rest of your essay, write an introduction. Then use your prewriting notes to explain how your evidence supports your main idea in clear, detailed sentences.

A strong opening sentence may be in the form of:

- An exclamation—*It feels awful when someone doesn't believe you!*

- A question—*Do you ever feel like your parents think you're still a baby?*

- A statement—*Hot water can scald you—but so can being accused of something you didn't do.*

Now write a rough draft of your introduction. A great introduction to an essay should get the reader's attention with a strong opening sentence, introduce the reader to your main idea, and summarize how you are going to support your main idea.

_____

_____

_____

_____

_____

_____

_____

_____

_____

_____

Use this page if you need more space.

_____

_____

_____

_____

_____

_____

_____

_____

_____

_____

_____

_____

_____

_____

_____

_____

_____

_____

_____

_____

_____

_____

Writing to Explore

Prewriting Notes

Think of a person you admire or look up to and something that person usually does—an action, habit, or routine—that you can describe in detail.

The person you admire: _____

Something this person does: _____

_____

In the boxes, write down each step of the person's action and some interesting details about it.

First,

Detail 1:

Detail 2:

Then,

Detail 1:

Detail 2:

Then,

Detail 1:

Detail 2:

Detail 1:

Detail 2:

Detail 1:

Detail 2:

Writing to Explore

Writing a Draft

Using your prewriting notes, write a description of the person you admire performing a task or action. Remember to include details when you describe the action he or she performs. Give your description a catchy title.

_____

_____

_____

_____

_____

_____

_____

_____

_____

_____

_____

_____

_____

_____

_____

_____

The Invisible Child

Tove Jansson

In the space below, write a keeper question about the story that came into your mind during the first reading, while sharing questions, or even right now. Choose one that no one has completely answered yet, and keep it in your mind during the second reading. If you still have the question after reading, continue to think about it—you picked a real keeper!

Your keeper question:

_____

_____

_____

_____

Visualizing helps you create pictures in your mind as you read a story. These pictures could come from any of your five senses (seeing, hearing, touching, tasting, or smelling) and how a passage makes you feel. It's like seeing a movie or a play in your mind.

- Find two passages you marked with a **V** and write down the page and paragraph numbers in the space below.

- Read the passage, close your eyes, visualize the scene, and write down what you see in your mind. Remember to consider all five senses and how the passage makes you feel.

- Reread the passage, close your eyes, and visualize the scene again.

- Describe how your image changed or became more detailed after rereading.

A passage you marked with a V: paragraph _____; page _____

The picture you see:

_____

_____

_____

_____

How your picture changed after rereading the passage:

_____

_____

_____

_____

A passage you marked with a V: paragraph _____; page _____

The picture you see:

_____

_____

_____

_____

How your picture changed after rereading the passage:

_____

_____

_____

_____

Head in the Clouds

Use your imagination! Choose one of the topics in the clouds and draw a picture or write a little bit more about the story.

A picture of Ninny once she becomes visible

A picture of the Moomins making apple-cheese

A page from Ninny's diary

What I would do if I were invisible

Building Your Answer

The focus question:

_____

_____

_____

_____

Your answer before the discussion:

_____

_____

_____

_____

Your answer after the discussion _(you may change or add to your first answer):_

_____

_____

_____

_____

_____

Writing to Explain   Concluding an Essay

Prewriting Notes

Use the web below to write down your answer and supporting evidence.
Then you'll be ready to write your introduction and your conclusion.

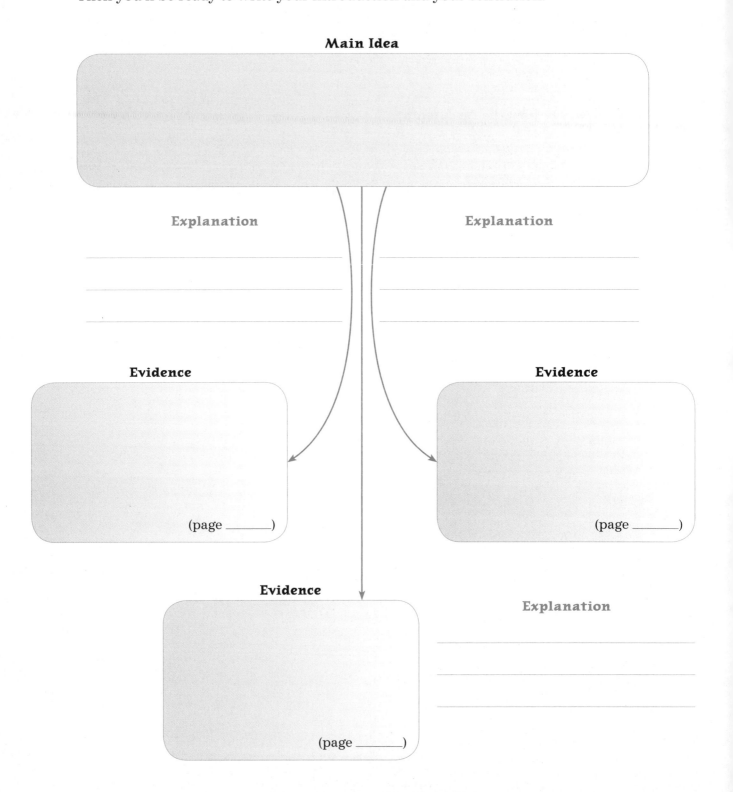

Main Idea

Explanation

_____

_____

_____

Evidence

(page _____)

Evidence

(page _____)

Evidence

(page _____)

Explanation

_____

_____

_____

Writing to Explain

Concluding an Essay

Write the introduction to your essay below.

Your introduction:

_____

_____

_____

_____

Your essay's conclusion should remind readers of your answer to the focus question and explain why your idea is important to understanding the story. Practice writing a conclusion below.

Your conclusion:

_____

_____

_____

_____

Writing to Explain

Writing a Draft

Now draft your essay, beginning with the introduction and ending with the conclusion you wrote on the previous page. You can use the web on page 70 to write the body of the essay.

_____

Introduction ─────────────────────────────────

_____

_____

_____

_____

Body
(2 or 3 paragraphs) ──────────────────────────────

_____

_____

_____

_____

_____

_____

_____

_____

_____

_____

_____

continue ⟶

Writing to Explain   Concluding an Essay

_____

_____

_____

_____

_____

_____

_____

_____

_____

_____

_____

_____

_____

_____

_____

_____

_____

_____

Conclusion _____

_____

_____

_____

Prewriting Notes

Imagine a person who is transformed so that the way he or she is on the *inside*—his or her personality—is expressed on the *outside*.

What is this person like on the *inside*?

_____

What might this person be like on the *outside*?

Detail 1: _____

_____

_____

_____

_____

Detail 2: _____

_____

_____

_____

_____

Detail 3: _____

_____

_____

_____

_____

Writing a Draft

Using your prewriting notes, write a description of your character, explaining what he or she is like on the inside and what he or she is like on the outside. Use as much detail as you can. Remember to include an interesting title!

_____

_____

_____

_____

_____

_____

_____

_____

_____

_____

_____

_____

_____

_____

_____

_____

_____

Use this page if you need more room.

_____

_____

_____

_____

_____

_____

_____

_____

_____

_____

_____

_____

_____

_____

_____

_____

_____

_____

_____

In the Time of the Drums

Gullah folktale
as told by Kim L. Siegelson

In the space below, write a keeper question about the story that came into your mind during the first reading, while sharing questions, or even right now. Choose one that no one has completely answered yet, and keep it in your mind during the second reading. If you still have the question after reading, continue to think about it—you picked a real keeper!

Your keeper question:

_____

_____

_____

_____

Read the passage below. Then close your eyes and visualize the scene.
Make a list of the words in the passage that helped you visualize.

Passage from the Story	List of Descriptive Words
"Mentu could scoot to the top of a live oak faster than a brush-tail squirrel. Could lift an iron skillet above his head with one hand, even though he still wore shirttails." (page 80)	

Now look in the story for a place that you marked with a **V** and copy the passage below. Make a list of the words in the passage that helped you **visualize**, and explain to a partner how those words helped you.

Passage You Marked with a V	List of Descriptive Words
(page _____)	

Head in the Clouds

Use your imagination! Choose one of the topics in the clouds and draw a picture or write a little bit more about the story.

A letter from Mentu to Twi

A story or lesson my family has taught me

A picture or description of what Twi's homeland might look like

A picture or description of Twi leading the people into the water

Building Your Answer

The focus question:

_____

_____

_____

_____

Your answer before the discussion:

_____

_____

_____

_____

Your answer after the discussion (_you may change or add to your first answer_)**:**

_____

_____

_____

_____

To support your answer, write two quotes or brief passages from the text.

1. _____

_____

_____

2. _____

_____

_____

Writing to Explain   A Developed Essay

Prewriting Notes

Fill in the evidence web below.

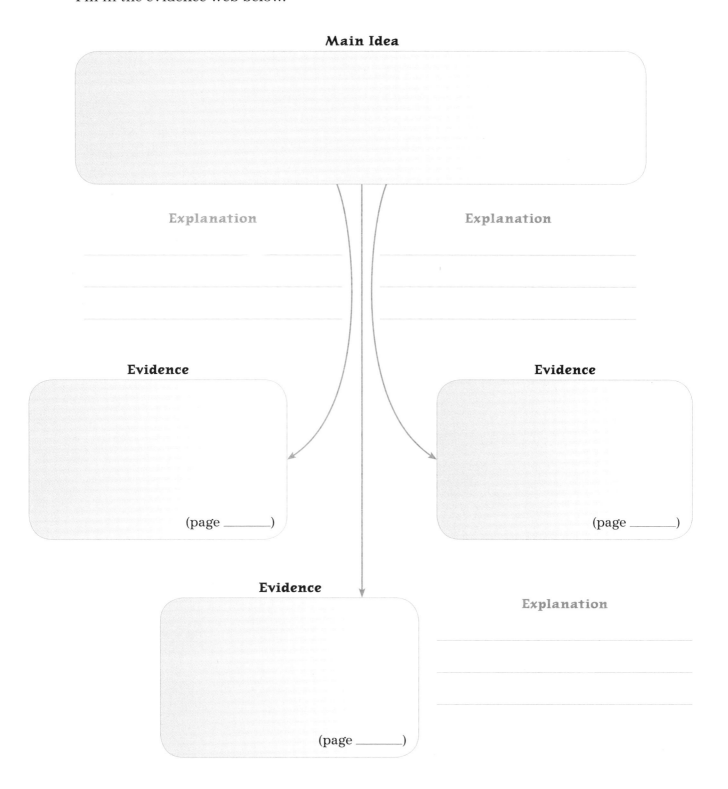

Main Idea

Explanation

Explanation

Evidence

(page _____)

Evidence

(page _____)

Evidence

Explanation

(page _____)

Writing to Explain

A Developed Essay

Now think of some ideas that will help you write an introduction and a conclusion for your essay.

Ideas for an introduction:

_____

_____

_____

_____

_____

_____

Ideas for a conclusion:

_____

_____

_____

_____

_____

_____

_____

Writing to Explain

A Developed Essay

Writing a Draft

Use the web to write the body of your essay, using clear, detailed sentences. Also include an introduction and a conclusion. Give your essay a title that will capture the reader's attention, offering the reader some idea about the topic.

_____

Introduction _____

_____

_____

_____

_____

Body
(2 to 3 paragraphs) _____

_____

_____

_____

_____

_____

_____

_____

_____

_____

_____

_____

continue ⟶

Writing to Explain   A Developed Essay

_____

_____

_____

_____

_____

_____

_____

_____

_____

_____

_____

_____

_____

_____

_____

_____

_____

_____

Conclusion _____

_____

_____

_____

_____

Writing to Explore   Mapping Your Stories

Prewriting Notes

Draw your own map of a special place. It can be a place from when you were little or a place that you live in or visit now. Make an **X** and write a few descriptive notes next to each spot where important memories lie.

Writing to Explore   Mapping Your Stories

Writing a Draft

Choose one of the **X**s that you marked on your map and retell your memory in the space below, giving it an interesting title.

_____

Learning the Game

Francisco Jiménez

In the space below, write a keeper question about the story that came into your mind during the first reading, while sharing questions, or even right now. Choose one that no one has completely answered yet, and keep it in your mind during the second reading. If you still have the question after reading, continue to think about it—you picked a real keeper!

Your keeper question:

_____

_____

_____

_____

Visualizing helps you create pictures in your mind as you read a story. These pictures could come from any of your five senses (seeing, hearing, touching, tasting, or smelling) and how a passage makes you feel. It's like seeing a movie or a play in your mind.

- Find two passages you marked with a **V** and write down the page and paragraph numbers in the space below.

- Read the passage, close your eyes, visualize the scene, and write down what you see in your mind. Remember to consider all five senses and how the passage makes you feel.

- Reread the passage, close your eyes, and visualize the scene again.

- Describe how your image changed or became more detailed after rereading.

A passage you marked with a V: paragraph _____; page _____

The picture you see:

_____

_____

_____

_____

_____

How your picture changed after rereading the passage:

_____

_____

_____

_____

_____

A passage you marked with a V: paragraph _____; page _____

The picture you see:

_____

_____

_____

_____

_____

How your picture changed after rereading the passage:

_____

_____

_____

_____

_____

Head in the Clouds

Use your imagination! Choose one of the topics in the clouds and draw a picture or write a little bit more about the story.

A part of the story that I feel strongly about

A picture of Gabriel standing up to Díaz

Something that the story reminds me of

A picture of the boys playing kick-the-can

Building Your Answer

The focus question:

_____

_____

_____

_____

Your answer before the discussion:

_____

_____

_____

_____

Your answer after the discussion (_you may change or add to your first answer_):

_____

_____

_____

_____

To support your answer, write two quotes or brief passages from the text.

1. _____

_____

_____

2. _____

_____

_____

Writing to Explain

What Is the Theme?

Prewriting Notes

One theme of the story "Learning the Game" is:

_____

_____

_____

_____

A **theme** is a major idea in a story. A theme goes beyond the characters and events in the story. It has to do with the story's overall meaning or with something important the author is trying to say.

On the next page, write your theme and evidence from the story that supports it. Then, after making sure your evidence is clear, write how each piece of evidence supports your theme in the space provided.

Writing to Explain   What Is the Theme?

Main Idea

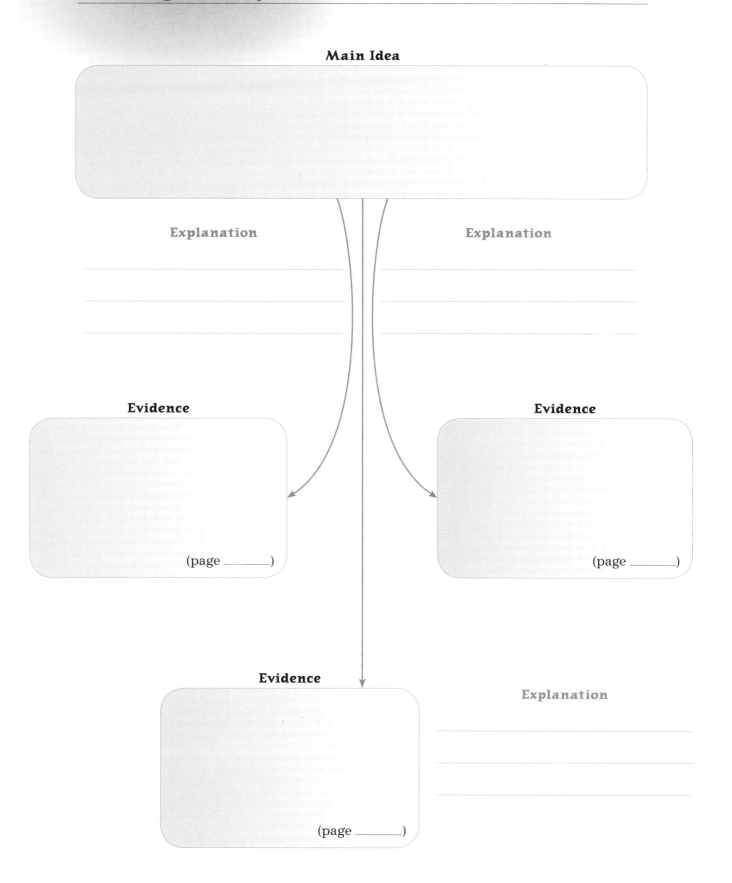

Explanation

Explanation

Evidence

(page _____)

Evidence

(page _____)

Evidence

(page _____)

Explanation

Writing to Explain What Is the Theme?

Writing a Draft

Use your prewriting notes to draft an essay about what you think one theme
of the story is. Convince your readers by choosing and explaining evidence from
the story. Write your draft using all the parts of an essay: title, introduction,
body, and conclusion.

_____

Introduction _____

_____

_____

_____

Body
(2 to 3 paragraphs) _____

_____

_____

_____

_____

_____

_____

_____

_____

_____

Page 94   **Learning the Game**

Writing to Explain

_____

_____

_____

_____

_____

_____

_____

_____

_____

_____

_____

_____

_____

_____

_____

_____

_____

_____

_____

_____

_____

Conclusion _____

_____

_____

_____

_____

Writing to Explore

Prewriting Notes

This letter is to (circle one):   Panchito   Gabriel

Below, list some ideas for your letter. Use the ideas on the board or create some of your own.

Writing a Draft

Write your first letter in the space below. Don't forget to include a salutation and a closing.

_____ ,

Writing to Explore

Writing a Reply

Your Name _____

After you have read your partner's letter, take some notes about how you, as Panchito or Gabriel, might respond.

Now write your reply in the space below.

_____ ,

_____

_____

_____

_____

_____

_____

_____

_____

_____

The Bat-Poet

Randall Jarrell

In the space below, write a keeper question about the story that came into your mind during the first reading, while sharing questions, or even right now. Choose one that no one has completely answered yet, and keep it in your mind during the second reading. If you still have the question after reading, continue to think about it—you picked a real keeper!

Your keeper question:

_____

_____

_____

_____

You have practiced asking **questions**, making **connections**, and **visualizing** while reading. Review your notes and choose one passage that you marked with a **?**, one you marked with a **C**, and one you marked with a **V**. Below, explain how you used each strategy. Then choose *one* strategy and explain how it helps you understand the story better.

The passage marked with a **?** is on page _____, paragraph _____.

Your question about this passage:

_____

_____

_____

_____

The passage marked with a **C** is on page _____, paragraph _____.

Your connection to this passage:

_____

_____

_____

_____

The passage marked with a **V** is on page _____, paragraph _____.

What you visualize while reading this passage:

_____

_____

_____

_____

How does your question, connection, **or** visualization (circle one) **help you understand something in the story?**

_____

_____

_____

_____

_____

Head in the Clouds

Use your imagination! Choose one of the topics in the clouds and draw a picture or write a little bit more about the story.

A picture or description of the chipmunk

My own poem about the little brown bat

A sentence from one of the poems that I liked, and why

A picture or description of the mockingbird driving the other animals away

Building Your Answer

The focus question:

_____

_____

_____

_____

Your answer before the discussion:

_____

_____

_____

_____

Your answer after discussion _(you may change or add to your first answer)_:

_____

_____

_____

_____

_____

_____

Include another answer you heard in discussion that supports yours.

_____

_____

_____

_____

_____

_____

Writing to Explain   The Chipmunk's Day

Prewriting Notes

Listen as your leader reads "The Chipmunk's Day" aloud. Underline the imagery in the poem.

> **Imagery** in a poem or story is the language that helps you form pictures in your mind as you read.

The Chipmunk's Day

In and out the bushes, up the ivy,
Into the hole
By the old oak stump, the chipmunk flashes.
Up the pole.

To the feeder full of seeds he dashes,
Stuffs his cheeks,
The chickadee and titmouse scold him.
Down he streaks.

Red as the leaves the wind blows off the maple,
Red as a fox,
Striped like a skunk, the chipmunk whistles,
Past the love seat, past the mailbox,

Down the path,
Home to his warm hole stuffed with sweet
Things to eat.
Neat and slight and shining, his front feet

Curled at his breast, he sits there while the sun
Stripes the red west
With its last light: the chipmunk
Dives to his rest.

Now look at the poem and outline the right-hand side of the poem. Read the poem to yourself and notice how the outline helps you see the poem's shape as you read.

Writing a Draft

Draft an essay answering this question:

Why does the chipmunk say, "Oh, it's nice. It goes all in and out, doesn't it?"
(page 111) *after he hears the bat's poem about him?*

Persuade your readers of your answer by using parts of the poem as evidence and the notes you just made about imagery and shape in the poem. Be sure to explain how your evidence supports your main idea. Write your draft using all the parts of an essay: title, introduction, body, and conclusion.

_____

Introduction _____

_____

_____

_____

_____

Body
(2 to 3 paragraphs) _____

_____

_____

_____

_____

_____

_____

_____

_____

continue ⟶

The Chimpmunk's Day

_____

_____

_____

_____

_____

_____

_____

_____

_____

_____

_____

_____

_____

_____

_____

_____

_____

Conclusion _____

_____

_____

_____

_____

Writing to Explore   An Animal Poem

Prewriting Notes

Your animal: _____

Think of a few *similes* to describe an animal and write them in the
organizers below.

A **simile** is a poetic comparison of two different things using the
word *like* or *as*. For example, the bat uses this simile to describe
the chipmunk:

Red ∕as∖ the leaves the wind blows off the maple

Writing to Explore

An Animal Poem

Now think of some *onomatopoeia* that describe your animal.

Onomatopoeia is using a word that sounds like the thing or action
it describes. Some of the words the bat uses in his poem about the
mockingbird—*cheeping, squeaking, shrieking, meowing*—are examples
of onomatopoeia.

_____   _____

_____   _____

_____   _____

_____   _____

_____   _____

Writing to Explore   An Animal Poem

Writing a Draft

Write a poem about your animal. Include some of the similes and onomatopoeia from your prewriting notes, and give your poem a title.

Writing Notebook

This is your chance to look back at what you have written in your Reader's Journal, choose a piece you wrote that you like, and make it the best that it can be. Here's how to revise your draft:

1. Choose the Writing to Explain piece you wrote that you would most like to revise.

2. Mark the page with a paper clip or a sticky note and turn in your Reader's Journal to your teacher.

3. Look at page 112 in this section of your Reader's Journal. Read and think about your teacher's note. Review the story and your Reader's Journal for more ideas.

4. Plan your revised draft in the prewriting notes section (page 113, 117, or 121). Then write your revised draft in the space on the next page.

Writing Notebook

The piece you plan to revise is about one of these stories (circle one):

The No-Guitar Blues   Kaddo's Wall   Turquoise Horse

It is on page _____ of the Reader's Journal.

From Your Teacher

Think about your teacher's note to help you make your writing shine.

_____ **Make the main idea clearer.**

Teacher's note: _____

_____

_____

_____ **Give more evidence to support the main idea.**

Teacher's note: _____

_____

_____

_____

_____ **Explain more about how your evidence supports the main idea.**

Teacher's note: _____

_____

_____

_____

Page 112 **Writing Notebook**

Prewriting Notes

Use a web, a chart, or a list to plan your writing.

Writing Notebook

Use this page if you need more room.

Writing Notebook

The piece you plan to revise is about one of these stories (circle one):

A Game of Catch   Oliver Hyde's Dishcloth Concert   The Hundred-Dollar Bill

It is on page _____ of the Reader's Journal.

From Your Teacher

Think about your teacher's note to help you make your writing shine.

_____ **Give more evidence to support the main idea.**

Teacher's note: _____

_____

_____

_____ **Choosing which story events are important and explain why.**

Teacher's note: _____

_____

_____

_____ **Make your introduction clearly explain the main idea and how you will support it.**

Teacher's note: _____

_____

_____

_____ **Make your introduction stronger to catch the reader's attention.**

Teacher's note: _____

_____

_____

Prewriting Notes

Use a web, a chart, or a list to plan your writing.

Writing Notebook

Your Revision

Page 118   Writing Notebook

Use this page if you need more room.

_____

_____

_____

_____

_____

_____

_____

_____

_____

_____

_____

_____

_____

_____

_____

_____

_____

_____

_____

_____

_____

_____

Writing Notebook

The piece you plan to revise is about one of these stories (circle one):

The Invisible
Child

In the Time
of the Drums

Learning
the Game

The Bat-Poet

It is on page _____ of the Reader's Journal.

From Your Teacher

Think about your teacher's note to help you make your writing shine.

_____ **Make your conclusion clearer to remind the reader of your answer
to the focus question.**

Teacher's note: _____

_____

_____

_____ **Explain clearly in your conclusion why your answer is important to
understanding the story.**

Teacher's note: _____

_____

_____

_____ **Give more evidence from the story to explain the main idea.**

Teacher's note: _____

_____

_____

_____ **Explain how each piece of evidence supports the main idea.**

Teacher's note: _____

_____

_____

Writing Notebook

Prewriting Notes

Use a web, a chart, or a list to plan your writing.

Use this page if you need more room.

Curious Words

For each story, write down a curious word and the page number where the word appears. Then do one of the following—or make up a fun way to use the word yourself!

- Write why you like your curious word, why it seems curious to you, or why you remember it.

- Pretend that one of the characters in a story uses your curious word and write down something the character says.

- Use your curious word in a message—for example, in a birthday or a friendship card, in a poem, or in a funny note to a friend.

Curious Words

"The No-Guitar Blues"

Your curious word: _____ page _____

_____

_____

_____

_____

Your curious word: _____ page _____

_____

_____

_____

_____

Your curious word: _____ page _____

_____

_____

_____

_____

Curious Words

"Kaddo's Wall"

Your curious word: _____ page _____

_____

_____

_____

_____

Your curious word: _____ page _____

_____

_____

_____

_____

Your curious word: _____ page _____

_____

_____

_____

_____

Curious Words

"Turquoise Horse"

Your curious word: _____ page _____

_____

_____

_____

_____

Your curious word: _____ page _____

_____

_____

_____

_____

Your curious word: _____ page _____

_____

_____

_____

_____

Curious Words

"A Game of Catch"

Your curious word: _____ page _____

_____

_____

_____

_____

Your curious word: _____ page _____

_____

_____

_____

_____

Your curious word: _____ page _____

_____

_____

_____

_____

Curious Words

"Oliver Hyde's Dishcloth Concert"

Your curious word: _____ page _____

_____

_____

_____

_____

Your curious word: _____ page _____

_____

_____

_____

_____

Your curious word: _____ page _____

_____

_____

_____

_____

Curious Words

"The Hundred-Dollar Bill"

Your curious word: _____ page _____

_____

_____

_____

_____

Your curious word: _____ page _____

_____

_____

_____

_____

Your curious word: _____ page _____

_____

_____

_____

_____

Curious Words

"The Invisible Child"

Your curious word: _____ page _____

_____

_____

_____

_____

Your curious word: _____ page _____

_____

_____

_____

_____

Your curious word: _____ page _____

_____

_____

_____

_____

Curious Words

"In the Time of the Drums"

Your curious word: _____ page _____

_____

_____

_____

_____

Your curious word: _____ page _____

_____

_____

_____

_____

Your curious word: _____ page _____

_____

_____

_____

_____

Curious Words

"Learning the Game"

Your curious word: _____ page _____

_____

_____

_____

_____

Your curious word: _____ page _____

_____

_____

_____

_____

Your curious word: _____ page _____

_____

_____

_____

_____

Curious Words

"The Bat-Poet"

Your curious word: _____ page _____

_____

_____

_____

_____

Your curious word: _____ page _____

_____

_____

_____

_____

Your curious word: _____ page _____

_____

_____

_____

_____

Glossary

In this glossary, you'll find definitions for words that you may not know, but that are in the stories you've read. You'll find the meaning of each word as it is used in the story. The word may have other meanings as well, which you can find in a dictionary if you're interested. If you don't find a word here that you're wondering about, go to your dictionary for help.

abstract: An **abstract** work of art uses lines, shapes, or colors to represent an idea, a feeling, or a physical object.

abstractedly: When you do something **abstractedly**, you do it while lost in thought. The boy stared **abstractedly** out of the bus window, paying no attention to his classmates.

accomplished: Something is **accomplished** when it is done skillfully and usually involves a lot of practice. The paintings at the school's art exhibition were all **accomplished**, showing a deep understanding of color, light, and perspective.

accustomed: When you are **accustomed** to something, you are used to it. You should be **accustomed** to regular after-school practice if you are on a sports team.

affront: An insult that is meant to hurt someone's feelings or pride. It was an **affront** to the honest boy when the manager accused him of stealing and banned him from the store.

anticipating: When you **anticipate** something, you prepare for it in your mind. **Anticipating** the first day of summer vacation, we made plans to swim, bike, and go fishing.

apron: The paved strip of concrete in front of a building.

arroyo: A deep, narrow valley cut into the earth by a stream.

attentively: Paying close attention. The children watched the magician **attentively** to try to figure out his tricks.

authoritative: Someone who is **authoritative** has the power to give orders or may just pretend to have that power. The crossing guard's **authoritative** manner made the children obey her directions.

awe: A feeling of great wonder and respect, sometimes mixed with a little fear. You might be in **awe** of your teacher because she always seems to know when students are misbehaving behind her back.

awkward: When something is **awkward**, it is clumsy or not graceful. The newborn calf took its first **awkward** steps toward its mother.

barrack: A building where workers and their families live or where soldiers live.

basque: The part of a dress that covers a woman's body from the shoulders to the waist. In the past when it was used, a **basque** usually fit tightly and was worn on special occasions.

bass: The lowest male singing voice. A man with a **bass** voice can sing the lowest notes in a song.

beckoned: When you **beckon** to someone, you signal to that person, asking him or her to come to you. My mother **beckoned** to me when we got separated by the crowd.

bewildered: If you are **bewildered**, you are puzzled or confused. The boy was **bewildered** trying to find his classroom on his first day at a big, new school.

bewitchedly: Describes something done in a charmed or enchanted manner. The girl listened to her pet canary's **bewitchedly** cheerful song.

biff: A hit or a punch. Your older sister might give you a **biff** on the shoulder if you were to make fun of her.

bitterness: A deep, long-lasting anger that comes from feeling wronged or that something is unfair. You might have **bitterness** if your friend beat you in an essay-writing contest and you know that he cheated. The girl felt great **bitterness** at having her sticker collection stolen right from under her nose.

bobbed: When you **bob** your head and shoulders, you move them up and down in a quick gesture, often out of respect. When the customer entered the fancy restaurant, the waiter **bobbed** and said, "Right this way, sir."

bracero: A Spanish word for a farm worker from Mexico who works in the United States for short periods of time.

brake: An area overgrown with dense trees and bushes.

briary: A patch of ground with many prickly shrubs and bushes.

burden: Something heavy that you carry or serious responsibility that is often hard to deal with. The student was happy to set down the **burden** of his overstuffed backpack. Lifeguards have the **burden** of preventing people from drowning, sometimes risking their own lives to rescue others.

calico: A kind of cloth with brightly colored designs.

calloused: An area of the skin that has become hardened is **calloused**. If you went barefoot every day in summer, the bottoms of your feet would become **calloused**, so you could walk on gravel or hot pavement without pain.

casting: An object formed by pouring hot, melted material into a mold and allowing it to harden. A **tufa-casting** is a special kind of casting where the mold is made from *tufa*, which is a type of stone.

chanterelles: Edible mushrooms that are orange or yellow and trumpet shaped.

charity: Kind feelings for others or willingness to help them. After finding a burglar in their house, the family showed **charity** by inviting him to dinner instead of calling the police.

cheerio: A friendly way of saying "goodbye!" or "see you later!"

chickadee: A small gray bird with black markings on the top of its head and under its beak. The **chickadee** has a call that sounds like its name.

chorizo con huevos: Spanish for *sausage with eggs.*

cinnamon: A reddish brown spice originally from Sri Lanka and surrounding areas. People bake **cinnamon** in muffins and cakes, and sprinkle it in oatmeal.

circumstances: The conditions that affect an event or a place are its **circumstances.** It's 70 degrees outside and sunny; under those **circumstances,** we won't be going sledding. No **circumstances** (rain, sleet, hail, or angry dogs) will make our mail carrier skip his delivery route.

clenched: To **clench** is to squeeze together or tighten. Your teeth might be **clenched** when you're angry.

climax: The most exciting or dramatic part of a story or event, usually happening near the end. The **climax** of a wedding ceremony might happen when the minister tells the groom, "You may kiss the bride."

composed: When you have **composed** something (such as a song or a story), you created it using your imagination. Between the years 1590 and 1613, William Shakespeare **composed** thirty-seven plays.

composure: A state of calmness and peace. A person with great **composure** is calm and has control over his or her emotions. The girl's **composure** during the fire helped her get out of the house without freezing in fear.

concentrate: Pay attention and keep focused. You would have to **concentrate** hard to be a tightrope walker in the circus. The boy had trouble **concentrating** on what his aunt was saying to him because he couldn't stop looking at her funny hat.

confession: In the Catholic church, **confession** is a time when people tell their sins to a priest.

conjunto **music:** A kind of music popular in Texas and Mexico. It features an accordion and a kind of guitar called a *bajo sexto.* ***Conjunto*** is Spanish for *together.*

conjure: To make someone or something appear or happen by doing magic. The magician lifted his top hat to show us a rabbit he had **conjured** out of thin air. A **conjure woman** heals people or helps them with other requests using magic.

contentedly: When you do something **contentedly**, you do it in a happy and satisfied way. You might sigh **contentedly** after enjoying a big, delicious meal.

contratista: A Spanish word that means "contractor," a person who agrees to work for someone else in exchange for money.

cordially: In a respectful and polite way. Your teacher and your parents might speak **cordially** to one another at parent-teacher night—or at least you hope they will!

corset: A tight undergarment worn by women to shape the waist and hips. The old-fashioned **corset** laced up in the back and had to be tied at the top in the same way you would tie your shoelace.

crocheted: Something that's **crocheted** is made with thread or yarn that has been looped together with a hooked needle. My grandma made a **crocheted** sweater.

cultivating: You **cultivate** crops when you care for them so that they grow. The farmers are **cultivating** strawberries to sell at the market.

dawdling: When you **dawdle**, you take more time than necessary or do something very slowly. You might **dawdle** in front of a movie theater, deciding whether to see the afternoon show.

deceitful: Someone who is not honest or who lies to others is **deceitful**. If you tried to sell some used pens to your classmates by telling them the pens were new, you would be a **deceitful** salesperson. The **deceitful** girl crashed her brother's bike and then told him she didn't know how the bike got dented.

decent: Good, thoughtful, and kind. It was **decent** of my teacher to lend me her umbrella during the thunderstorm.

deliberation: Doing something with **deliberation** means doing it carefully and slowly, paying attention as you go. When you say something with **deliberation**, you've thought about the words and really mean what you say. If you were gluing a broken pot back together, you might fit the pieces together with **deliberation** to make sure they stay.

delicate: Describes something that is finely made. The threads of a spider's web are **delicate**. The **delicate** vase was so thin that you could almost see through it.

determined: If you are **determined** to do something, you have made a firm decision to do it. You might be **determined** to finish all of your homework on Saturday morning so that you can have fun with your friends in the afternoon.

dignity: A sense of self, pride, and honor. You might lose a game of checkers with **dignity** by complimenting your opponent on a good game. If some kids were making fun of you, you might keep your **dignity** by walking away calmly rather than letting them see you were upset.

discouraged: If you are feeling **discouraged**, you have lost hope or confidence. The girl couldn't do a handstand no matter how much she practiced, and she was beginning to get **discouraged**. If you lost the spelling bee three years in a row, you might become **discouraged** and not want to compete anymore.

dissolved: When something **dissolves**, it disappears or melts into a liquid form. The hot tea made the sugar **dissolve** quickly. After the storm, the clouds slowly **dissolved** and the sun appeared.

distracted: Someone who is **distracted** is not paying attention. If you are **distracted** in class, you may be looking out the window or talking with a friend rather than learning the lesson. It's easy to become **distracted** from your homework if you're trying to watch television at the same time.

dreary: When something is **dreary**, it is boring and a little gloomy. Cleaning the basement can be a **dreary** task, especially if there are other things you'd rather be doing.

drowsily: Sleepily or in a half-asleep way. If you stay up late to finish your homework, you might get up slowly and **drowsily** the next morning.

dutifully: If you do something **dutifully**, you do it obediently because you know you should do it. When it's your turn to clean up after dinner, you might wash the dishes **dutifully,** even though you'd rather be playing.

dwindling: When something **dwindles**, it slowly becomes smaller. When a candle is about to burn out, the flame begins **dwindling** down until it is gone.

eaves: The part of a roof that hangs over the side of a building. Sparrows and other birds often build nests underneath the **eaves** of a house.

eerie: Something that is strange or spooky is **eerie**. Some people think a wolf's howl is **eerie** because it has a sad, echoing sound.

effective: When something is **effective**, it makes something happen that you wanted to happen, or it produces a strong response. An **effective** ghost story might send chills down your spine.

egrets: see **snowy egrets**

elegant: Graceful, beautiful, or of fine quality. The wedding guests drank water from **elegant** crystal glasses.

empanada: A kind of pastry with a meat or vegetable filling.

entranced: If you are **entranced**, you are so caught up in something that you stop what you're doing or forget to pay attention to what's around you. Everyone was so **entranced** by the movie that they didn't hear the doorbell ring.

eroded: When something is **eroded**, that means it has been gradually worn away by water or wind. The Grand Canyon is **eroded** where water has flowed through it for millions of years, wearing away the rock to form a deep valley.

etched: To **etch** something, you draw on metal or glass using a sharp object or acid to cut through the surface, making lots of small lines.

exaggerated: When something is **exaggerated**, it seems bigger, better, greater, or more than it really is. If a cat sees an unfriendly dog, it might puff out its tail to **exaggerate** its size. We all knew his story about catching a hundred fish was **exaggerated** because he hardly knows how to use a fishing pole.

exclaimed: Something said suddenly because you were surprised or excited. "Stop!" the policeman **exclaimed** as the robber ran down the street.

exuberant: High-spirited or full of joy. The **exuberant** girl hugged her friend, yelling, "I got the lead part in the play!"

fabulous: Something **fabulous** is so amazing that it is hard to believe. People say a unicorn lives in the forest, but no one has ever seen the **fabulous** animal.

famine: In a **famine**, there is an extreme lack of food, and people starve because they don't have enough to eat.

fascinating: Something that is very interesting and holds your attention is **fascinating**. We listened eagerly to the mountain climber's **fascinating** story of climbing Mount Everest.

fidgeted: To **fidget** is to move around in an uneasy or nervous way. The girl **fidgeted** in her seat until her father told her to keep still.

fixedly: Holding steady and firm. If you are staring **fixedly** at something, you are keeping your eyes on it, not blinking much or moving your head.

flailed: When you **flail**, you wave or swing something with big movements. The boy **flailed** his arms and legs as he fell backwards into the pool.

flank: An animal's **flank** is its side, between its ribcage and its hip.

flybane: A kind of poisonous mushroom that is red with white spots.

forehooves: The front hooves of an animal that has four legs.

fretful: Describes something that causes you to feel uneasy, or someone who is feeling worried. The baby's **fretful** crying kept me awake all night. Your mother might become **fretful** if you were two hours late getting home from a friend's house.

fringed: Something that is **fringed** has a border around its edge. The pillows were **fringed** with bright yellow ribbons.

gave: To **give** is to move or break under force or pressure. The door **gave** a little when I pushed against it.

generous: If you are **generous**, you are willing and happy to share the things you have with others. She is very **generous** with her toys and lets other children play with them all the time. The **generous** man always invited the whole neighborhood to his parties.

gladiolus: A kind of garden plant with sword-shaped leaves and a long spike of brightly colored flowers.

gnats: Small winged insects that live off blood or plant juices.

granary: A building for storing grain.

gravelly: When a sound is **gravelly**, it is low, rough, and sometimes unpleasant. The cheerleader's voice is always **gravelly** after a long football game.

grindstones: A **grindstone** is a round, flat stone that can be used to sharpen or shape tools. **Grindstones** are also used to crush grain into a powder.

Groke: A creature who lives in the imaginary land of Moominvalley.

guitarron: A large bass guitar.

harried: Someone who is **harried** feels stress from trying to do too much or from being bothered by lots of questions or demands. The **harried** mother was trying to unlock the door, while carrying in two bags of groceries and listening to her children's endless questions.

heeled in: To **heel in** a tree is to plant it for the time being while you prepare its permanent home. The gardener dug a shallow hole and placed a cherry tree in it, covering the roots loosely with soil to keep the tree **heeled in**.

hijo: Spanish for *son*.

hogan: A Navajo house, usually built of logs or branches and covered with earth.

homeland: The place or country where you were born and that you think of as your true home. Although the boy's grandmother has lived in the United States for fifty years, Mexico is her **homeland**.

horrid: Ugly, unpleasant, or nasty. Our **horrid** neighbors yell at us if we play too close to their house. Rotten eggs have a **horrid** smell.

huaraches: Sandals with flat heels and woven leather straps. **Huaraches** are popular in Mexico and the southwestern United States.

hüerquito: A Spanish word that adults use to address children. It means *little one* or *silly one*.

hull: A ship's **hull** is the framework or body below its deck. The luxury ship *Titanic* sank after its **hull** hit an iceberg.

humanity: All people in the world, or the human race. The basic needs of **humanity** are food, water, and shelter. For the good of **humanity**, it's best not to pollute the oceans.

iambic foot: A rhythm used in poetry. An **iambic foot** is two syllables long and has an accent on the second syllable when you say it out loud. *Today*, *for now*, *delight*, and *the best* are examples of **iambic feet**.

iambic pentameter: A line of poetry that has five *iambic feet*, or ten syllables. *The yellow spider crawling up the wall* is an example of a line of **iambic pentameter**.

iambic trimeter: A line of poetry that has three *iambic feet*, or six syllables. *I cannot sleep tonight / The moon is shining bright* are two lines of **iambic trimeter**.

icily: In a cold, unfriendly way. Since our big fight, my best friend stares **icily** at me whenever she sees me.

ideal: When something is **ideal**, it is perfect or the best it can be for a given person or situation. The start of the school year is an **ideal** time to buy new school supplies.

imitate: To copy someone or something. If you wanted to **imitate** your friends, you might copy their voices and how they walk.

immobile: When you are **immobile**, you are not moving a muscle. When you're playing hide-and-seek, it's important to stay **immobile**, because any movement could give you away.

inaudible: Not loud enough to be heard. The radio was turned down so low that it was **inaudible**.

indistinguishable: When people or things are **indistinguishable**, you can't tell the difference between them. The twins liked to make themselves **indistinguishable** by dressing exactly alike. Some brightly colored butterflies are **indistinguishable** from the flowers they land on, which makes it hard to see them.

indolently: When you do something **indolently**, you do it in a lazy way, without trying very hard. If you wash the windows **indolently**, you sweep over them once with a cloth without making them much cleaner.

infallible: Guaranteed not to fail. The bank robbers got away with all the money in the safe, thanks to their **infallible** plan.

intently: When you do something **intently**, you focus on what you're doing and give it your full attention. Basketball players look at the basket **intently** when they are about to shoot a free throw. You might read a good story so **intently** that you don't even notice the other people in the room.

introductory: Something that is **introductory** gives you your first experience of something and hopefully makes you want more. The new hardware store's **introductory** offer is a free toolbox with every purchase.

jolting: Sudden jerking or bumping. The **jolting** of the car along the bumpy road made me feel sick.

jouncing: When you **jounce**, you bounce or make bumping, jerking movements. You might try to annoy your parents by **jouncing** up and down on the sofa and making the springs creak.

juniper: A **juniper** is a small evergreen tree, usually with pale blue-gray berries.

keel: A **keel** is the long beam along the bottom of a boat that holds it together. A boat that is turned **keel** upward is upside down.

kerosene: A thin, colorless liquid that is used to light nonelectric lamps.

latillas: Straight branches or poles pushed together to form a rooflike covering that provides shade from the sun.

lector: Someone who reads aloud during a church service.

leech: A kind of worm that lives in water or moist earth. Most leeches survive by attaching themselves to an animal and then sucking its blood or flesh. If you describe someone as being a **leech**, that person uses others for his or her gain, but never gives anything back in return.

lichen: A life form made up of fungi and either green algae or cyanobacteria, or sometimes both. Some **lichens** look like moss or a thin crust; others look like cabbage leaves, pale fingers, or delicate ropes.

lob: To throw something high into the air. You might **lob** a tennis ball for your dog to catch.

luxurious: Something **luxurious** gives you great pleasure and delight because of how beautiful or high-quality it is. She went on vacation and stayed in a **luxurious** hotel with a giant pool and room service.

magnificently: When something is done **magnificently**, it's done in a way that is splendid, grand, or very beautiful. The dancer leaped **magnificently** into the air and landed on one foot.

mandolin: A small musical instrument with strings and a pear-shaped body.

mangy: Worn out and dirty. The old cat who lives in the alley has **mangy** fur and a cut on one ear.

mannered: When something is **mannered**, it's done as though it has been practiced or planned out in advance. If you were to behave in a **mannered** way, you would act as though you had a script for what you were doing or saying. Our waiter said, "Good evening, ladies and gentlemen" in a very **mannered** way.

marmalade: A jelly made from oranges or other citrus fruit.

meadowlark: A kind of bird known for its musical calls.

meditative: If you are in a **meditative** mood, you are thinking deeply and quietly. You might feel **meditative** when you are resting in a quiet room or strolling early in the morning.

melancholy: Sad and gloomy. You might feel **melancholy** if your best friend moved away.

menacing: Threatening or dangerous. Because of the **menacing** storm clouds, the teachers decided to move the class picnic into the gym.

mesa: A hill or mountain with a flat top and steep sides.

millet: A kind of grain that has small, round seeds. **Millet** can be boiled and eaten or used to make flour or beer.

mimicked: To copy someone or something in order to make fun of them. The children **mimicked** the teacher, not realizing he was standing just outside the doorway and could hear every word.

mincer: A machine that chops food into very small pieces.

misery: A feeling of suffering and great unhappiness. If your pet ran away and you couldn't find it, you might feel **misery**. The flood caused **misery** for many people because it destroyed everything they had and forced them to leave their homes.

mockingbird: A gray and white songbird that can imitate the calls of other birds.

modest: People who are **modest** don't show off or brag about their talents, possessions, or achievements. If you were **modest** about being a good speller, you might just say thank you when people compliment you.

monopolizing: When you are **monopolizing** something, you are controlling it or keeping it all to yourself. The boy talked on and on, **monopolizing** the conversation so that no one else could speak.

mortar: Usually made of cement, sand, and water, **mortar** is used to hold bricks or stones in place, and gets very hard when it dries.

mournful: Very sad. The girl was **mournful** after the loss of her pet.

muffled: When a sound is **muffled**, it seems quieter or softer than normal. If you were to talk with a blanket over your head, your voice would sound **muffled**.

muscular: Having strong, well-developed **muscles**.

muslin: A kind of cotton cloth, used especially to make sheets, curtains, and clothing.

negligent: If you are **negligent** about something, you are careless about it or you pay no attention to it. If you are **negligent** about taking care of your dog, you might not remember to feed or walk it until bedtime.

oilskin: Cloth that has been treated with oil to make it waterproof.

overseer: Someone who watches and directs workers.

panicky: Extremely alarmed or scared. The **panicky** sheep ran back and forth across their pen while the dog barked at them from behind the fence.

papas: Spanish for *potatoes*.

peremptory: When you say someone has a **peremptory** manner, it means that that person is self-confident and doesn't leave room for argument/other people's opinions. The teacher said in a **peremptory** way, "I don't care what your excuse is—your homework is still due today."

permitted: Allowed. You are probably not **permitted** to leave school grounds during the day without a written excuse.

perpetual clock: A clock that keeps perfect time longer than most clocks. A **perpetual clock** winds itself according to changes in air pressure and temperature.

perplexed: Confused or puzzled. After losing the instructions, she was **perplexed** about how to assemble the model airplane.

personage: A person of high rank. The crowd was excited for the queen's visit because such a well-known **personage** had never come to their village before.

petticoats: A **petticoat** is a thin skirt worn underneath a dress or outer skirt.

pews: Benches that people sit on in church.

piped: Spoke in a shrill, high tone of voice. The child **piped**, "I will be in kindergarten next year."

pitching: Something is **pitching** if it is moving up and down or back and forth with great force. The tall stack of boxes kept **pitching** forward and falling over.

placket: A cut made in a piece of clothing to make movement easier.

plantation farms: Large farms found in warm-weather areas where crops such as coffee, tea, rubber, and cotton are grown. Before it was made illegal in the nineteenth century, many people were enslaved and forced to work on **plantation farms** in the United States.

porcelain: A type of pottery that is hard and white. You can see through **porcelain** if you hold it to the light.

possum: A **possum** (short for **opossum**) is a small furry mammal that lives in trees and carries its young in a pouch. When threatened, the **possum** lies very still, as if it were dead.

queer: Odd or strange. I can't explain it, but I have a **queer** feeling that school will be canceled tomorrow.

range: The distance between certain points is called a **range**. You can hear sounds in a **range** from very soft, like a whisper, to very loud, like a clap of thunder. If you have a good vocal **range**, you can sing both high notes and low notes.

rapture: Great happiness, joy, or delight. As the bus pulled up to the gates of the amusement park, the boy felt **rapture** at the thought of going on all the rides. My little sister was in **rapture** when she got a hermit crab for her birthday.

reluctantly: Acting in a way that shows you don't really want to do what you are doing. If you are having fun at a party, you are probably going to leave **reluctantly**. I returned the boy's basketball **reluctantly**, because I was in the middle of a game.

remedies: A **remedy** is something that relieves pain or discomfort, or cures sickness. There are lots of **remedies** for getting rid of hiccups, but my favorite is to drink a glass of water without stopping to breathe.

responsive: When you are **responsive** to something, you are able to understand and appreciate it. A **responsive** student might ask and answer lots of questions to show that she understands the lesson.

restlessly: If you are doing something **restlessly**, you are doing it without keeping still or paying attention very well. If you are pacing **restlessly**, you're probably walking back and forth quickly, stopping every so often.

rhyme scheme: The pattern of rhyming sounds at the end of lines in a poem. The **rhyme scheme** of my poem is very simple: each line ends with a word that rhymes with *dog*.

righteous: A **righteous** person does things that are good, honest, and moral. If you were to find a wallet full of cash, returning it would be the **righteous** thing to do. Many **righteous** people in the nineteenth century fought to end slavery because they believed it was wrong.

roan: Reddish-brown with flecks of gray or white, usually describing hair or animal fur. The **roan** horse grazed peacefully in the field.

scalded: Burned with very hot liquid or steam. You might get **scalded** in the shower if you turn the cold water all the way off but leave the hot water running. The woman was **scalded** with soup when she knocked the pot off the stove.

scrubby: Covered with low bushes, brush, or short, skinny trees. **Scrubby** can also mean run-down or shabby.

sensitive: Being highly aware of your surroundings and of what others say and do. The **sensitive** girl felt terrible when her mother forgot to hang her art project on the refrigerator. If your eyes are **sensitive** to bright light, you might keep the window blinds closed on sunny days.

serene, serenely: Something **serene** is calm and peaceful. A baby who is fast asleep looks very **serene**. You might float **serenely** in a lake on a warm, beautiful day.

sharecropper: Someone who lives and farms on land that is owned by someone else, and who gives a set portion of the crops to the landowner as rent.

shimmered: When something **shimmers**, it shines with a soft, flickering light. The candles **shimmered** in our neighbor's window.

shindigs: A **shindig** is a lively party with music and dancing. The mayor always hired a band for the town's Fourth of July **shindigs**.

shortly: When you say something **shortly**, you say it quickly, often in a rude or unfriendly way. If your little brother keeps pestering you to play with him, you might say **shortly**, "Go away!"

shrieking: Loud, sharp screaming. The strong wind made a **shrieking** noise around the house during the storm.

silversmith: A person who makes or repairs silver objects.

sin vergüenza: A Spanish phrase that means "scoundrel."

snout: The long front part of an animal's head, including the nose, mouth, and jaw. My dog poked his wet **snout** into my hand, hoping I had a treat for him.

snowy egrets: Large, white, wading birds with long bills, necks, and legs.

snuff: A form of tobacco that is inhaled or chewed.

solemnly: When you do something **solemnly**, you do it very seriously. You might **solemnly** promise never to lie to your best friend. When we went to see Grandpa in the hospital, we listened **solemnly** as the nurse explained the visiting rules.

spindly: Long, thin, and rather weak. The plant's **spindly** stems couldn't support its large flowers.

splendid: Something **splendid** is very beautiful or excellent. The male peacock displayed its **splendid** feathers to attract the nearby female.

squinted: If you **squint** at something, you nearly close your eyes in order to see it. We **squinted** in the bright sun as we came out of the dark movie theater.

staid: A **staid** person is very proper and serious. I was **staid** and on my best behavior when my brother's boss came to dinner.

stale: When something is **stale**, it is no longer fresh. The basement smells **stale** because no one ever opens the windows.

stammered: To **stammer** is to speak in an unsure, halting way, stopping often and repeating certain sounds or words. The embarrassed student **stammered** an excuse for being late to class.

stanzas: Groups of two or more lines into which a poem or song is divided.

structure: Something that has been built, like a house, a building, a bridge, or a dam.

supple: Something **supple** bends and moves easily. A dancer has to have a **supple** body in order to stretch and leap into the air. The long, **supple** grass waved back and forth in the wind.

surplus: More of something than you need or can use.

swaggered: Walked in a bold, proud way. The team **swaggered** across the field after winning the baseball game. The older boy **swaggered** through the playground, daring others to fight with him.

taquitos: A Spanish word for flat corn or flour pancakes (*tortillas*) filled with slow-cooked ground meat or vegetables and then fried.

taunt: To try to make someone upset by mocking or teasing, or by doing something he or she can't do. You might **taunt** your little sister by holding her favorite toy just out of her reach.

technically: How someone handles the necessary skills for an activity such as art, music, or sports. I don't like her style of painting, but **technically**, she is a very good artist.

tentatively: To do something in an uncertain or hesitating way. If you think you know the answer to a question in class but aren't sure, you might raise your hand **tentatively**.

territory: A section or area of land that is held and defended by a government, an animal, or a person. The dog growled whenever another animal tried to enter its **territory**.

thrilling: Something **thrilling** gives you a sudden, strong feeling of excitement and pleasure, sometimes mixed with fear. Riding on a roller coaster can be **thrilling**, because it is enjoyable and scary at the same time.

timidly: Done in a shy or frightened way. You might say hello **timidly** to a group of strangers if you have trouble meeting new people.

titmouse: A small, insect-eating songbird.

transformed: When you **transform** something, you make a great change to it or change it into something else. The boy helped his mother paint the walls and set up a crib to **transform** the spare bedroom into a nursery for the new baby. A lump of clay can be **transformed** into a vase or a pot by an artist.

tremendously: Greatly or extremely. You might feel **tremendously** happy if you tried out for the school play and got a part.

trilling: A high-pitched musical hum that some birds, frogs, and insects can make. We couldn't sleep because we heard the cicadas **trilling** all night.

triumph: The joy you feel when you win or succeed at something. The girl smiled in **triumph** after winning the race. I felt great **triumph** when I baked my first cake. The basketball player made a jump shot at the buzzer and ran **triumphantly** across the court.

trooped: Moved, marched, or walked together as a group. I **trooped** across the street with my classmates because our teacher told us to stay together.

twittered: Made short, high, chirping sounds, like a bird. The robin **twittered** happily as it searched for worms.

uneasily: Doing something in a way that shows you feel worried or unsure. The man climbed the steps of the bus **uneasily** because of the cast on his leg.

uneasy: Worried or unsure. The girl felt **uneasy** about going to sleep after watching a scary movie on TV.

upright: When something is **upright**, it is standing or sitting up straight. She set the chair **upright** after accidentally knocking it down.

vapors: Thin mist, steam, or smoke. An airplane flying overhead leaves a trail of **vapors** in the sky.

vast: Huge or wide. If you go to a soccer game, you might be as impressed by the **vast** crowd of fans as you are by the game.

veranda: An open porch around the outside of a house, often enclosed under a roof. My aunt loves to drink iced tea on her **veranda**.

verge: The edge or border of something. The workers on the roof were comfortable walking near the **verge**.

verse: Words put together rhythmically in a pattern that often rhymes. William Shakespeare wrote his plays in **verse**.

vicinity: The area near or around a particular place, a neighborhood. I let my cats play outside as long as they stay in the **vicinity** of my house.

wash: A **wash** is the dry ground that shows when a stream or river stops flowing as heavily or dries up.

weathered: Aged, dried, or bleached by the weather. If people work in the sun for many years and don't wear sunscreen or a hat, they might have **weathered** skin.

whinnied: To **whinny** is to make a gentle neighing sound. The horse **whinnied** as I pulled off its saddle.

wretched: If you feel **wretched**, you are feeling unhappy, uncomfortable, or just plain awful. You might feel **wretched** if you broke your friend's new game and couldn't buy him a new one. The man had a **wretched** time getting his new boots off because they were too tight and had given him blisters.